Basketball
LEGENDS

Blaine Wiseman

AV² provides enriched content that supplements and complements this book. Weigl's AV² books strive to create inspired learning and engage young minds in a total learning experience.

Your AV² Media Enhanced books come alive with...

 Audio
Listen to sections of the book read aloud.

 Key Words
Study vocabulary, and complete a matching word activity.

 Video
Watch informative video clips.

 Quizzes
Test your knowledge.

 Embedded Weblinks
Gain additional information for research.

 Slide Show
View images and captions, and prepare a presentation.

 Try This!
Complete activities and hands-on experiments.

... and much, much more!

Go to **www.av2books.com**, and enter this book's unique code.

BOOK CODE

P 3 3 7 4 8 3

AV² by Weigl brings you media enhanced books that support active learning.

Published by AV² by Weigl
350 5th Avenue, 59th Floor
New York, NY 10118
Website: www.av2books.com

Library of Congress Control Number: 2016956742

ISBN 978-1-4896-4799-3 (hardcover)
ISBN 978-1-4896-5049-8 (softcover)
ISBN 978-1-4896-4800-6 (multi-user eBook)

Printed in the United States of America, in Brainerd, Minnesota
1 2 3 4 5 6 7 8 9 21 20 19 18 17

072017
310117

Project Coordinator: Jared Siemens
Designer: Terry Paulhus

Photo Credits
Every reasonable effort has been made to trace ownership and to obtain permission to reprint copyright material. The publisher would be pleased to have any errors or omissions brought to their attention so that they may be corrected in subsequent printings. The publisher acknowledges Getty Images and Newscom as its primary image suppliers for this title.

Basketball
LEGENDS

Contents

AV² Book Code 2

History and Culture 4

The NBA Finals 6

Basketball Equipment 8

Greatest Legends 10

Shooting and Blocking 12

Money Makers.....................................14

Arenas of North America......................16

Coaches and Officials 18

Most Valuable Players 20

Quiz..22

Key Words/Index 23

Log on to www.av2books.com..............24

History and Culture

The game of basketball was invented in 1891 by Dr. James Naismith, a teacher in Springfield, Massachusetts. In 1898, the National Basketball League (NBL) was formed. This was the first professional basketball **league**. Basketball's popularity spread quickly. By the early 1900s, it was played all over the United States. In 1946, a **rival** league formed. It was called the Basketball Association of America (BAA). The two leagues competed against each other until 1949, when they merged to form the National Basketball Association (NBA).

Dirk Nowitzki is a basketball player who was born in Germany. He joined the Milwaukee Bucks in 1998. Today, he plays for the Dallas Mavericks.

Men's basketball was first included in the Summer Olympics in 1936. Since then, the U.S. men's team has won 14 gold medals in Olympic basketball, more than any other country in history.

Courtside

In the NBA, the best seats are right on the floor, in the front row, at court level. These seats, called courtside seats, are difficult to get, and can cost large amounts of money. It is common to see celebrities cheering on their favorite teams from courtside seats. Film directors Spike Lee and Woody Allen are two of the best-known courtside faces at Knicks games. These fans pay thousands of dollars each game to sit in courtside seats.

Pickup Basketball

Basketball can also be enjoyed outdoors. Many parks in cities around the world have become venues for games of three-on-three, five-on-five, 21, horse, and many other types of basketball games. The NBA hosted an outdoor game in San Juan, Puerto Rico, between Milwaukee and Phoenix in 1972. The next outdoor NBA game was held in 2008, when the Suns played the Denver Nuggets in a **preseason** game at the Indian Wells Tennis Garden in Indian Wells, California.

Mascot Madness

Mascots are an entertaining part of basketball games. Crazy characters run around the arena, exciting the fans and performing stunts. Sometimes, mascots become part of the game. In 2009, during a playoff game between the Atlanta Hawks and the Miami Heat, Atlanta's mascot, a real hawk named "Spirit," was released to fly around the stadium. Spirit would not stop flying around, and the game had to be delayed.

The NBA Finals

The Golden State Warriors defeated the Cleveland Cavaliers in Game Five of the 2017 NBA Finals for its second Finals win in three years.

The first basketball playoff in the United States took place in 1947, when two teams in the BAA played against each other for the championship. The Philadelphia Warriors, who won the 1947 playoff series, are considered to be the first winners of the NBA Finals. In 1949, the BAA and the NBL merged to create the NBA, and the format of the game changed.

Today, 30 teams make up the NBA. They spend the 82-game season trying to win games in order to become world champions in basketball. Each spring, the NBA playoffs end when one team wins the championship game. This team is presented with the Larry O'Brien NBA Championship Trophy.

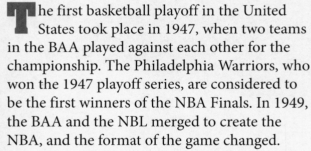

The Larry O'Brien Trophy is made of sterling silver covered in gold. It is made to look like a life-size basketball on the edge of a basket. The trophy weighs about 16 pounds (7.3 kilograms), and it stands 2 feet (0.6 meters) tall.

NBA FINALS RECORDS

8 TITLES — Between 1959 and 1966, The Boston Celtics won the most consecutive **NBA Championship titles.**

8 APPEARANCES — Elgin Baylor of the Los Angeles Lakers has the **most championship appearances without a win.**

11 WINS — Bill Russell of the Boston Celtics has **won the most championships** of any player in NBA history.

455 FREE THROWS — Over his career, Jerry West made **more free throws** during the NBA Finals than any other player in NBA history.

61 POINTS — Elgin Baylor **scored the most points** of any player in a championship game.

Championship History

Since their first title in 1957, the Boston Celtics have won championships in every decade except the 1990s. The Celtics have won more titles than any other team. They won 10 titles in the 12 years between 1957 and 1969. The Celtics record-setting 17th league championship came in 2008, when they defeated the Los Angeles Lakers. With 16 titles, the Lakers are second on the list of teams with the most championship titles.

NBA FINALS WINNERS

Boston Celtics

Los Angeles Lakers

Chicago Bulls

Golden State Warriors

San Antonio Spurs

17

16

6

5

5

Basketball Equipment

The basketball equipment used today is very different from the equipment used when the game first began in 1891. Over time, as the game gained popularity, technology improved the ball, the hoops, the uniforms, and even the courts. Today, the NBA sets official equipment guidelines for professional basketball teams.

UNIFORM
The first basketball players wore long, baggy pants, and long, buttoned jerseys. Today's uniforms feature sleeveless shirts and long, baggy shorts that are designed to keep players cool. Every uniform features the team's logo and colors, as well as the name and number of the player.

NBA teams wear dark or colored uniforms when they play away from their home arena.

The home team wears white uniforms. If neither team is in a home arena, then the second team on the schedule wears the white home uniforms.

BASKETBALL

Naismith invented basketball using other sports for inspiration. At first, players used a soccer ball. Soon, people began making special balls by stitching leather around a rubber **bladder**. Molded basketballs were first made in the 1940s, and are still used today. These balls are made in a factory from a mold, which makes each ball exactly the same. This allowed players to become more skilled at the sport because every ball bounces the same.

SNEAKERS

Basketball sneakers combine style with function. Originally, basketball players wore low-cut **canvas** shoes. Starting in the 1920s, Chuck Taylors became the most popular basketball shoe. These shoes were made of canvas with rubber **soles**. In 1972, Nike changed the look and structure of basketball shoes with a more supportive shoe featuring many different styles. Some offer ankle support or extra cushioning, which help with running and jumping.

NET

The first basketball games were played using peach baskets as nets. This is why the sport was named basketball. With each point that was scored, the janitor at Naismith's school would climb a ladder to retrieve the ball from the basket. In 1892, a metal wire **rim** replaced the peach baskets. Open-bottom nets were added to the wire rims in 1912.

Greatest Legends

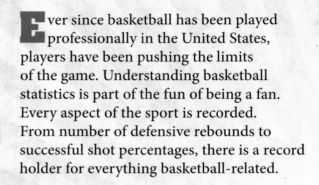

Ever since basketball has been played professionally in the United States, players have been pushing the limits of the game. Understanding basketball statistics is part of the fun of being a fan. Every aspect of the sport is recorded. From number of defensive rebounds to successful shot percentages, there is a record holder for everything basketball-related.

Michael Jordan

Michael Jordan was one of the most exciting, effective basketball players of all time. He led the Chicago Bulls to six NBA championships and broke many records throughout his career, including the number of points in a playoff game. He was also the leading scorer in the history of the All-Star Game. "Air Jordan" is best known for his **dunking** ability and his dependable shooting.

Tamika Catchings

Tamika Catchings first started playing basketball in high school, where she became the first person to score a quintuple double. This means that Catchings achieved a double-digit total number of points, rebounds, assists, steals, and blocked shots in a single game. Since joining the Women's National Basketball Association (WNBA) in 2001, Catchings has gone on to set and break many records. She was an All-Star 10 times, more than any other WNBA player. Catchings has also played on the U.S. women's Olympic basketball team, and has won four gold medals.

Kareem Abdul-Jabbar

Kareem Abdul-Jabbar was **drafted** to the Milwaukee Bucks in 1969, and made a name for himself in the NBA record books. Over the course of his 20-year NBA career, he scored the most points, with more than 30,000. He was also named Most Valuable Player (MVP) six times during his career, the most of any player in NBA history.

7 ft.

6 ft.

5 ft.

4 ft.

Assists

Play makers assist their teammates in scoring by passing the ball. They also control the flow of the offense. These players are the NBA's leaders in all-time career assists.

John Stockton 15,806

Jason Kidd 12,091

Steve Nash 10,335

Most-Awarded MVP

In 1956, the NBA created the MVP award. One player is named MVP every season. These players hold the highest number of MVP awards.

PLAYER	MVP AWARDS
Kareem Abdul-Jabbar	6
Michael Jordan	5
Bill Russell	5

3 ft.

Tallest

Successful basketball players are often tall. The average height in the NBA is about 6 feet 7 inches (1.9 m). These are the tallest athletes to have played in the NBA.

2 ft.

Muggsy Bogues holds the record for being the shortest NBA player. He is 5 feet 3 inches (1.6 meters) tall. During his first year in the NBA, Muggsy was on the same team as Manute Bol, one of the NBA's tallest players.

1 ft.

PLAYER	HEIGHT
Manute Bol	7 feet 7 inches (2.3 meters)
Gheorghe Muresan	7 feet 7 inches (2.3 meters)
Shawn Bradley	7 feet 6 inches (2.28 meters)

Shooting and Blocking

Shaquille O'Neal is widely considered to be one of the top NBA players of all time. He was known for his ability to dunk the ball.

Stephen Curry began his NBA career in 2009, and has played with the Golden State Warriors since then. He is often named as the best shooter in NBA history.

Though basketball teams can have up to 15 players, only 5 can play at a time. There are five main positions on a basketball team. The first is the point guard. This player calls plays, directs other players, and is responsible for passing the ball. The second is the shooting guard. This player's job is to shoot from the outside of the key and score points. The third and fourth positions are the small forward and power forward. Small forwards are fast, and are important for both defense and offence. The power forward, or post, stands just underneath the basket, and is mostly used in offense and rebounding. The final player is the center, who is usually the tallest player on the team. This player must be able to play all positions, from scoring on the inside, to blocking in defense.

Blocks

A block is an important defensive play in basketball. It stops a basket, and can turn the game around for the defensive team. These players hold the all-time blocking records.

PLAYER	BLOCKS
Hakeem Olajuwon	3,830
Dikembe Mutombo	3,289
Kareem Abdul-Jabbar	3,189

Steals

In basketball, stealing is an effective play. When players make a steal, their team turns from defense to offense. These players have the most career steals.

PLAYER	STEALS
John Stockton	3,265
Jason Kidd	2,684
Michael Jordan	2,514

Rebounds

When a basketball hits the rim or the backboard, players jump up to grab the ball before the other team can get it. This is called a rebound. Here are the best rebounders of all time.

PLAYER	REBOUNDS
Wilt Chamberlain	23,924
Bill Russell	21,620
Kareem Abdul-Jabbar	17,440

Most Points Scored

38,387 Kareem Abdul-Jabbar

36,928 Karl Malone

33,643 Kobe Bryant

32,292 Michael Jordan

31,419 Wilt Chamberlain

John Stockton was a 10-time NBA All-Star. He was known for his commitment to his team. The Utah Jazz made the playoffs every year during his 19-year career with the team.

Money Makers

The NBA is a huge business. The average value of an NBA team is more than $1 billion. Currently, the NBA is the third most valuable sports league in the world. Only the National Football League and Major League Baseball are worth more. In 2016, the NBA's 30 teams brought in a revenue of about $5.9 billion. Today, the average basketball fan spends close to $100.00 at a basketball game.

SOFT DRINK
$4.00

HOT DOG
$5.00

TICKET
$55.00

HAT
$30.00

TOTAL
$94.00

Business of Basketball

People pay billions of dollars to own NBA teams. These teams can make their owners very rich. The top five most valuable teams in the NBA are listed below.

$3.3 BILLION	New York Knicks
$3 BILLION	Los Angeles Lakers
$2.6 BILLION	Golden State Warriors
$2.5 BILLION	Chicago Bulls
$2.2 BILLION	Boston Celtics

Signing Bonus

NBA salaries work on a scale. The earlier a player is drafted, the higher his salary. Teams may also offer players signing bonuses. Unlike many other sports, however, the NBA has placed a limit on how large a signing bonus can be. Today, a signing bonus must be no higher than 15 percent of a player's annual salary.

Sporting Salaries

Many professional basketball players earn millions of dollars. Some of that money comes from sponsorships, but many players also receive large salaries. These athletes are currently paid the most money each year for playing basketball.

LeBron James
$30,963,450

Al Horford
$26,540,100

Mike Conley
$26,540,100

Carmelo Anthony
$24,559,380

Dirk Nowitzki
$25,000,000

Arenas of North America

The NBA uses 29 arenas across the United States and Canada for its games. Each arena is home to one of the 30 NBA teams. The Staples Center, in Los Angeles, is home to two teams. The venues that the NBA uses for basketball can also be used for other events, such as concerts or hockey games. Just like the players, some arenas stand out above the others. This map shows the location of some of basketball's best-known arenas in the United States and Canada.

UNITED CENTER
Chicago, Illinois

The United Center is the largest arena in the United States. It measures 960,000 square feet (89,186 square meters).

ORACLE ARENA
Oakland, California

The Oracle Arena was opened in 1966, and is the oldest NBA stadium still in use today.

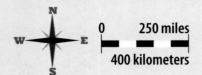

0 250 miles
400 kilometers

LEGEND
- United States
- Canada
- Water
- Other Countries

Pacific Ocean

British Columbia
Alberta
Washington
Oregon
Nevada
California
Utah
Colorado
Arizona
New Mexico
Texas

CANADA

UNITED STATES

MEXICO

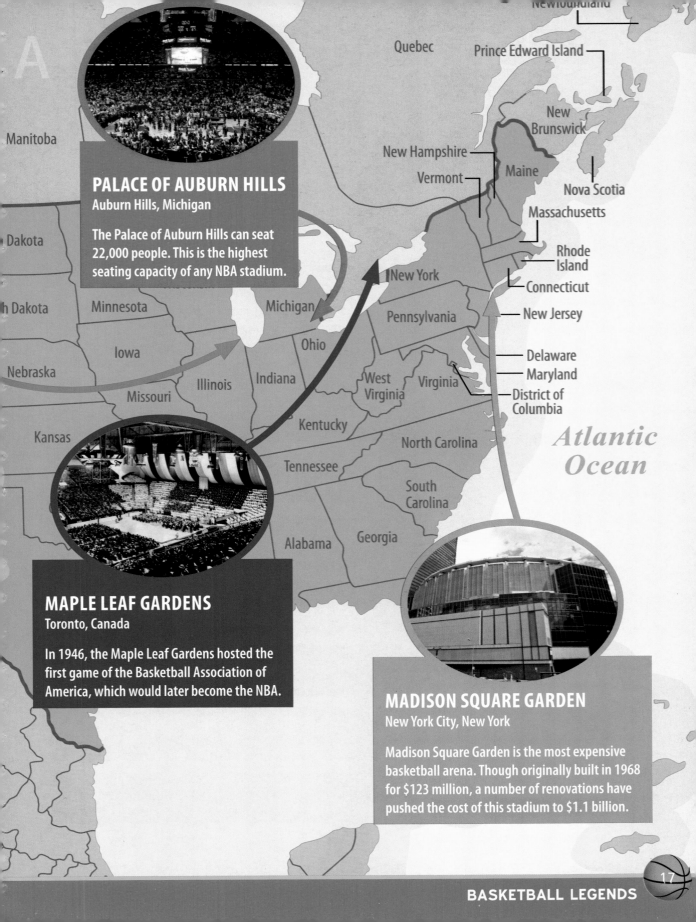

PALACE OF AUBURN HILLS
Auburn Hills, Michigan

The Palace of Auburn Hills can seat 22,000 people. This is the highest seating capacity of any NBA stadium.

MAPLE LEAF GARDENS
Toronto, Canada

In 1946, the Maple Leaf Gardens hosted the first game of the Basketball Association of America, which would later become the NBA.

MADISON SQUARE GARDEN
New York City, New York

Madison Square Garden is the most expensive basketball arena. Though originally built in 1968 for $123 million, a number of renovations have pushed the cost of this stadium to $1.1 billion.

Quebec
Prince Edward Island
New Brunswick
Manitoba
New Hampshire
Vermont
Maine
Nova Scotia
Massachusetts
Dakota
Minnesota
Michigan
Rhode Island
Connecticut
h Dakota
Iowa
Ohio
Pennsylvania
New Jersey
Nebraska
Illinois
Indiana
New York
Delaware
Maryland
Missouri
West Virginia
Virginia
District of Columbia
Kansas
Kentucky
North Carolina
Tennessee
Atlantic Ocean
South Carolina
Alabama
Georgia

Coaches and Officials

Each team has a head coach, who is in charge of training and practicing with the players. More and more of these positions are being filled by former talented players. The head coach is supported by assistant coaches, who each specialize in a specific area of the game, such as defense.

Phil Jackson

Phil Jackson, the current president of the New York Knicks, is the most successful coach in NBA history. Over his career, Jackson has won a record 70.5 percent of games he coached, and he holds the record for the most championship wins. In Chicago, Jackson coached the Bulls to six NBA championships. Jackson has also won more playoff games than any other coach.

Phil Jackson by the Numbers

$12 million	Salary
1,155	Games Won
229	Playoff Games Won
25	Years as Coach
11	Championships Won

Phil Jackson became a member of the Basketball Hall of Fame as a coach in 2007.

Jerry Sloan played for the Chicago Bulls before becoming the team's coach in 1979. In 1988, he became coach of the Utah Jazz.

Lenny Wilkens

Lenny Wilkens played in the NBA from 1960 to 1975. He began coaching while still playing for Seattle, and then later played and coached for Portland. Wilkens also coached in Cleveland, Atlanta, Toronto, and New York. He has won more career games than any other coach. Wilkens was **inducted** into the Basketball Hall of Fame twice. He was first inducted as a coach in 1988, and then as a player in 1989.

Most Games Won

Winning is the most important stat in basketball. With 82 games in the regular season, and 30 teams playing, racking up wins can get difficult. These coaches have won the most regular-season games in their NBA careers.

COACH	WINS
Don Nelson	1,335
Lenny Wilkens	1,332
Jerry Sloan	1,221

Most Seasons Coached

NBA coaches often hold their position for decades. However, coaches do not often stay with one team over their entire coaching career. These are the NBA coaches who have coached the longest.

COACH	SEASONS
Lenny Wilkens	32
Don Nelson	31
Larry Brown	26

Don Nelson is known as an innovator in basketball. He created the Nellie Ball, a play where smaller, faster forwards score points by outrunning their opponents.

Most Valuable Players

Each year, the Associated Press awards one basketball player the title of Most Valuable Player (MVP). The MVP is the player that is considered to be the biggest value to his team. Other things that are considered are a player's history of wins, and the number of games played during the season. These players have all been MVPs.

Stephen Curry

2015 AND 2016 MVP • POINT GUARD • GOLDEN STATE WARRIORS

Stephen Curry grew up surrounded by basketball. He is the son of NBA player Dell Curry. Curry played high school basketball, and continued on to play at Davidson College until he was drafted, right before his senior year. Curry became a back-to-back MVP playing for the Golden State Warriors in 2015 and 2016. In 2016, he broke the record for the most consecutive games without missing a 3-pointer, with 128 shots completed.

Kevin Durant

2014 MVP • SMALL FORWARD • GOLDEN STATE WARRIORS

Kevin Durant **declared** for the NBA draft after only one year playing with the Texas Longhorns at the University of Texas. In 2007, he was drafted by the Seattle SuperSonics, a team that later became the Oklahoma City Thunder. Durant was named MVP in 2014 while playing for the Thunder. That year, he started 81 games and scored an average of 10.5 points per game. Durant signed to the Golden State Warriors in 2016 and was named the NBA Finals MVP in 2017.

LeBron James

2009, 2010, 2012, 2013 MVP • SMALL FORWARD, POWER FORWARD, CENTER, SHOOTING GUARD • CLEVELAND CAVALIERS

LeBron James is widely considered to be one of the best basketball players in the game. In 2003, straight out of high school, James was drafted to the Cleveland Cavaliers as the first pick in the draft. He has been awarded the NBA MVP award four times. James is known for consistency, and has scored a career average of 27.2 points per game.

Derrick Rose

2011 MVP • POINT GUARD • NEW YORK KNICKS

Chicago native Derrick Rose was selected by the Chicago Bulls as the first pick in the 2008 draft. In 2011, Derrick Rose was awarded the MVP after playing in 81 games and scoring an average of 8.8 points per game. In 2012, Rose injured his knee, and he could not play for a year after surgery. Rose was traded to the New York Knicks for the 2016 season.

Kobe Bryant

2008 MVP • SHOOTING GUARD, SMALL FORWARD • LOS ANGELES LAKERS

When Kobe Bryant was drafted in 1996, he became the first-ever shooting guard to enter the NBA straight out of high school. Shortly after being drafted, Bryant was traded to the Los Angeles Lakers, and he played his entire 20-year career with them. Bryant broke many records, including being the youngest player to score 30,000 points. He was named MVP in 2008.

Dirk Nowitzki

2007 MVP • POWER FORWARD, CENTER • DALLAS MAVERICKS

Dirk Nowitzki was born and raised in Germany, and was drafted into the NBA in 1998. Though he had a rocky start to his NBA career, Nowitzki is now regarded as one of the greatest power forwards of all time. He was named MVP in 2007. That year, he made 8.9 rebounds per game and scored 24.6 points per game. In 2012, Nowitzki became the first non-American player to be awarded the Naismith Legacy Award.

Quiz

Now that you have read about basketball legends, test your knowledge by answering these questions. All of the information can be found in the text. The answers are also provided for reference.

1 In what year did James Naismith invent basketball?

A: 1891

2 Who has been given the most MVP awards?

A: Kareem Abdul-Jabbar

3 What is the oldest NBA stadium still in use today?

A: The Oracle Arena

4 What NBA team is the most valuable?

A: The New York Knicks

5 What two leagues merged to form the NBA?

A: The National Basketball League and the Basketball Association of America

6 Where was the first NBA game played?

A: At Maple Leaf Gardens, in Toronto, Ontario, Canada

7 How many Olympic gold medals has Tamika Catchings won?

A: Four

8 Before the modern basketball was invented, what kind of ball did players use to play basketball?

A: A soccer ball

Key Words

bladder: an object that holds liquid or air

canvas: a strong type of cloth

declared: to announce in an official or public way

drafted: when an amateur player joins a professional basketball team

dunking: when a player is pushing the ball down through the hoop, also known as a "slam dunk"

inducted: chosen to be admitted into a position or an organization

league: a group of sports teams that play each other for a championship

preseason: games used as tryouts or warmups before the regular season

rim: the circular metal hoop that a basketball must pass through to score a point

rival: a team or person who competes with another for the same goal

soles: the bottoms of shoes

Index

Abdul-Jabbar, Kareem 11, 13, 22

Basketball Association of America (BAA) 4, 6
basketballs 9
Bol, Manute 11
Bryant, Kobe 13, 21

Catchings, Tamika 10, 22
Curry, Stephen 12, 20

Durant, Kevin 20

Jackson, Phil 18
James, LeBron 20
Jordan, Michael 10, 11, 13

Madison Square Garden 17
Maple Leaf Gardens 17, 22
mascots 5

Naismith, Dr. James 4, 21, 22
National Basketball Association (NBA) 4, 5, 6, 7, 8, 10, 11, 12, 13, 14, 15, 16, 17, 18, 19, 20, 21, 22
National Basketball League (NBL) 4, 6
NBA Finals 6, 7
nets 9
Nowitzki, Dirk 4, 15, 21

Olympic Games 4, 10, 22
O'Neal, Shaquille 12
Oracle Arena 16

Palace of Auburn Hills 17
pickup basketball 5

Rose, Derrick 21

signing bonuses 15
sneakers 9
Stockton, John 11, 13

uniforms 8
United Center 16

Wilkens, Lenny 19

Log on to www.av2books.com

AV² by Weigl brings you media enhanced books that support active learning. Go to www.av2books.com, and enter the special code found on page 2 of this book. You will gain access to enriched and enhanced content that supplements and complements this book. Content includes video, audio, weblinks, quizzes, a slide show, and activities.

AV² Online Navigation

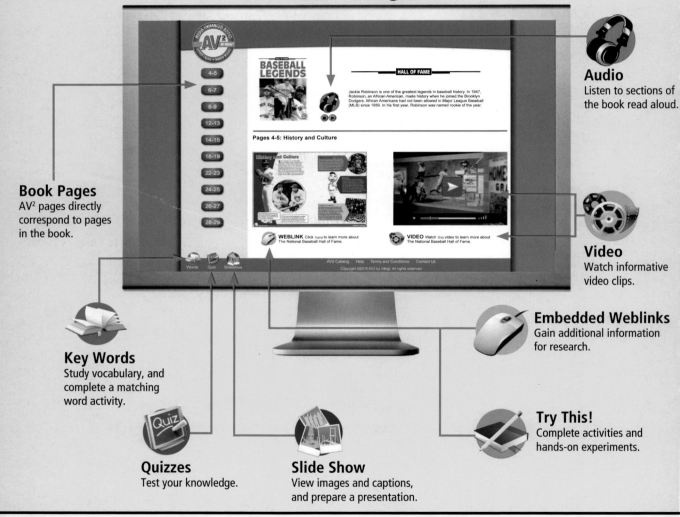

Audio
Listen to sections of the book read aloud.

Book Pages
AV² pages directly correspond to pages in the book.

Video
Watch informative video clips.

Key Words
Study vocabulary, and complete a matching word activity.

Embedded Weblinks
Gain additional information for research.

Quizzes
Test your knowledge.

Slide Show
View images and captions, and prepare a presentation.

Try This!
Complete activities and hands-on experiments.

AV² was built to bridge the gap between print and digital. We encourage you to tell us what you like and what you want to see in the future.

Sign up to be an AV² Ambassador at www.av2books.com/ambassador.

Due to the dynamic nature of the Internet, some of the URLs and activities provided as part of AV² by Weigl may have changed or ceased to exist. AV² by Weigl accepts no responsibility for any such changes. All media enhanced books are regularly monitored to update addresses and sites in a timely manner. Contact AV² by Weigl at 1-866-649-3445 or av2books@weigl.com with any questions, comments, or feedback.